7 Piano Duets &

inspired by music from around the world

John Pitts

Cover photo 'Sogni dei Santi', Le Marche, Italy © Charlie Groves 2016, used by permission.

About the author

John Pitts is a British composer who lives in Bristol, England, with his wife and four children. He composes mostly chamber music, especially for piano, in styles perhaps best summarised as melodic, motoric, motif-driven, jazz-tinged, post-minimal impressionism. His piano duets have been performed at a number of music festivals in several European countries, Ukraine and the USA, including in March 2015 a concert dedicated to his music in Perpignan's *"Festival Prospective 22ème siècle"* by French duo Émilie Carcy and Matthieu Millischer.

His 2009 album *Intensely Pleasant Music: 7 Airs & Fantasias and other piano music by John Pitts*, performed by Steven Kings, was released to critical acclaim - receiving a 5 star review in Musical Opinion Magazine, several 4 star reviews including the Independent newspaper, with descriptions such as *"beautiful, moving and relaxing"*, *"delicious"*, *"lovely"*, *"colossal… stunning and seriously impressive"*, *"great character and emotional integrity"*, *"exciting stuff all round… toes - prepare to tap."*

John studied at Bristol and Manchester Universities, under composers Wyndham Thomas, Adrian Beaumont, Raymond Warren, Geoffrey Poole, John Casken, John Pickard and Robert Saxton, and briefly with Diana Burrell in a COMA Composer Mentor scheme. He won the 2003 Philharmonia Orchestra Martin Musical Scholarship Fund Composition Prize at the Royal Festival Hall in London, and two of his chamber pieces were shortlisted by the Society for the Promotion of New Music. He has also written music for four plays and two short operatic works – *"Crossed Wires"* (Huddersfield Contemporary Music Festival 1997), and *"3 Sliced Mice"* (commissioned by Five Brothers Pasta Sauces). He writes music for Christian worship, with two hymns on Naxos CDs recorded by his eldest brother composer Antony Pitts and Tonus Peregrinus, including one in Faber's The Naxos Book of Carols. In 2006 Choir & Organ magazine commissioned *"I will raise him up at the last day"* for their new music series.

John was the secretary of the Severnside Composers Alliance from its inception in 2003 until 2015, with a special interest in music for piano triet by living composers. His own first triet *"Are You Going?"* (*"a toccata boogie of unstoppable, unquenchable verve"* Jonathan Woolf, MusicWeb International) was premiered at the 2010 Kiev Chamber Music Session Festival by the Kiev Piano Duo (with Antoniy Baryshevkiy), for whom he wrote *"Gaelic Faram Jig"* for 2 pianos and 2 percussionists for the 2012 festival. John has conducted four Bristol Savoy Operatic Society productions, arranging *Pirates of Penzance*, *Gondoliers* and *Iolanthe* for small band. In January 2010 he became the Associate Conductor of the Bristol Millennium Orchestra.

In 1994 he spent a gap year in Pakistan, which led to a number of chamber pieces heavily influenced by Indian classical music, including *"Raag Gezellig"*, a piano duet composed as the compulsory work for the Valberg International Piano 4 Hands Competition 2011, subsequently recorded by French duo Bohêmes (Aurélie Samani and Gabriela Ungureanu) and released by 1EqualMusic/Hyperion. Hearing that virtuosic Indian piano duet performed by a number of superb duos led to the desire to make Indian *raags* accessible to many more pianists, so please look out for his forthcoming book *"How to Play Indian Sitar Raags on a Piano"*.

www.johnpitts.co.uk

Welcome to this collection of 5 duets and 2 triets.

These 7 piano pieces were written between 1995 and 2015 for performers in UK, France and Denmark. They have the connecting thread of each being inspired by music of a different country. Four of the pieces have roots in traditional music - Indonesian gamelan, North Indian sitar raags, African balaphon ensembles, and British folksong – and the other three were inspired by German organ music (J.S.Bach), American minimalism and Spanish waltz (although it doesn't sound like it!).

Between them, they have been performed in festivals, concerts and international piano duo competitions in UK, Spain, France, Netherlands, Germany, Austria, Poland, Denmark, Norway, Estonia, Russia, Ukraine, Armenia and USA.

Most of the pieces are cheerful, vibrantly rhythmic and highly energetic, as well as requiring considerable dexterity. Find out a little bit about each piece over the next few pages.

ONE
"Changes for twenty nifty fingers" (1995) duet 3 minutes

This is the 'simplest' piece of the collection, and the oldest. I wrote it during my undergraduate years at Bristol University in response to a task set by my then composition tutor Wyndham Thomas. The given title *"Changes"* refers to the inspiration of the peeling of church bells – ringing the changes - where there is a simple ostinato pattern that undergoes a gradual metamorphosis. This piece starts with the skeleton of this short repeated phrase (in 14/8) which gradually fills out, and then moves through two enormously tricky sections of phasing - in which the two pianists have overlapping bars of different lengths (14 and 15 quavers). The duet finally builds to a dramatic climax in the third minute.

So, this is a short minimalist piece, ultimately with its technical roots in American minimalism, although the material was more immediately inspired by the piano style of my older brothers, in particular my eldest brother Antony's piano solo piece *Dance of the Redeemed Creation* - the style of which can be traced in many of my piano compositions.

Changes has been widely performed by the Kiev Piano Duo (Dmytro Tavanets and Oleksandra Zaytseva), and a recording (performed by Steven Kings and John Pitts) is available on CD "7 Airs & Fantasias and other piano music" from www.johnpitts.co.uk - or as a download from Hyperion/1equalmusic: www.hyperion-records.co.uk/dc.asp?dc=D_1EMIPM08

TWO
"Passacaglia" **(2000-2012) duet** 6 minutes

This piece also exists in versions for organ (my original version in 2000) and orchestra (performed by Bristol University Symphony Orchestra under the baton of John Pickard in 2001). The piano duet version was finally completed in 2012.

The theme is based on the ground bass from Bach's stonking *Passacaglia in C minor* for organ. However, the implied harmonies of Bach's original ground bass are treated to some "twisted harmonies" – where each chord is altered using a system of harmonic substitution - swapping each chord implication for a newly chosen one (Cm=C, Fm=F#, G=A, Dm=Ab, Eb=F and on it goes around the 12 chromatic notes).

Each key therefore has a 'dominant' and 'subdominant' that are not the actual chords V and IV in that key, so the traditional cadences and chord relationships are supplanted by 12 individual 3-chord relationships – one set of three chords for each of the 12 (now almost exclusively major) keys. In an attempt to recreate the pulls of the traditional tonic-dominant-subdominant relationships, each key then also has a particular mode/scale with particular added notes that are designed to recreate the sense of moving away from and back towards the home chord of that key. This results in a lot of rich added harmonies and some idiomatic voice-leading.

Bach's original theme in Cm is:
C G - Eb F - G Ab - F G - D Eb - B C - F G - C,

and in the opening statement of the ground bass this has become:
C A - E F# - A Bb - F# A - D# E - C# C - F# A - C.

There are then 21 variations which modulate through a range of keys, during which the ground bass is constantly re-adjusted to fit the new harmonic areas. It starts in C major, then goes through 'closely' related keys (eg A major and Ab major), and then back to C in variations 6, 9 and 11. This kind of arch then happens again but going through more distant keys before returning to C in variations 18, 19 and the final climactic variation 21.

Leaving aside the structural and tonal nuts and bolts, my aim was to compose a piece that attempts to recapture some of the nobility and beauty of Bach's *Passacaglia*, with rich added note harmonies, and exuding an exuberant joy.

THREE
"Raag Gezellig" **(2011) duet** 10 minutes

Raag Gezellig was composed at the request of French duo Mark Solé-Leris and Frédéric Chauvel as the compulsory contemporary work for the sixth International Piano 4 Hands Competition 2011 in Valberg, France. 'Gezellig' is a Dutch word with no precise English translation—the closest is probably 'cosy'—as in atmosphere (for example, with friends and a glass of wine around a fire). I've always liked the word and it seemed appropriate for an intimate piano duet. The piece becomes increasingly virtuosic—designed to test the professional duos' technical and musical skills to their limits—and stylistically draws heavily from the classical sitar *raag* (or *raga/rag*) tradition of Pakistan.

While *Raag Gezellig* is entirely through-composed, a traditional sitar *raag* is a semi-improvised form within a structure of three (or arguably four) sections:

1) the slow, pulseless *Alaap* introduction that gradually unveils the notes and melodic patterns of the raag over some low drone notes,
2) the pulsed, medium tempo *Jhor* section with its pre-composed melody (*gat*) that is interspersed with improvisations and variations, followed by a second *gat* at a faster tempo which leads into
3) the *Jhala* - the short, final section - very rhythmic and energetic with repeated high octave drone notes (the sitar's strummed *chikari* strings).

Raag Gezellig opens and closes with a gentle cascade, imitating a typical *raag*'s opening gesture - a descending glissando of the sitar's sympathetic strings. The rhythmically-free and quasi-improvised melody of the pulseless *Alaap* actually requires some rather complex-looking rhythmic notation - western notation is designed for music with a regular beat! The regular pulse and *tala* - a seven-beat rhythmic cycle - are introduced in the *Jhor* section, when you also hear the *gat* for the first time. One important feature is the *tihai* - where short phrases (of various lengths) are repeated three times before landing heavily on *sam* (beat 1 of the *tala*). There are numerous examples. The second *gat* is related to the first *gat* but with a faster tempo and different *tala* (seven quaver beats rather than seven crotchet beats). The final *Jhala*-inspired section gets going shortly afterwards at the same faster tempo.

Raag Gezellig has been widely performed in particular by French duo Bohêmes (Aurélie Samani and Gabriela Ungureanu) and recorded on their album "Harmonies d'un Soir" available from Hyperion/1equalmusic
www.hyperion-records.co.uk/dc.asp?dc=D_1EMHDUS

6

FOUR
"Joyful Balaphony" (2013) duet (prepared piano) 8 minutes

Joyful Balaphony was composed for French duo Émilie Carcy and Matthieu Millischer for a concert of duets/triet/quartets by John Pitts at Perpignan Conservatoire's *"Festival Prospective 22ème siècle"* 2015.
This duet was inspired by some traditional music from Burkina Faso in sub-saharan Africa - ensembles of balafons and djembes (hand-carved xylophones and drums).

The music is very percussive, obviously, with driving, pounding rhythms. Like a lot of other traditional musics, this african folk music is modal, and its timbres - the sounds - are both sweet and also unrefined.
There are some optional piano preparations which attempt to capture some of the exotic soundworld.

FIVE
"Glittering Gamelan" (2014) duet (prepared piano) 3 minutes

A short duet composed as an encore for Danish/British duo Ingryd Thorson and Julian Thurber for a concert in the 2014 Samsø Piano Festival, Denmark, which included three other duets in this collection.

It was inspired by a particular type of gamelan music from Indonesia - "Gamelan Balaganjur" - which translates as "Gamelan of Walking Warriors". This style of music has its historical origins in military music - music used in battle. These days it is performed in Indonesia in competitions by large bands of dancing musicians, with pitched and unpitched percussion. Their music is incredibly elaborate, and has very little repetition. It involves constantly changing speeds with layers of complex rhythmic gestures that require very impressive ensemble skill.

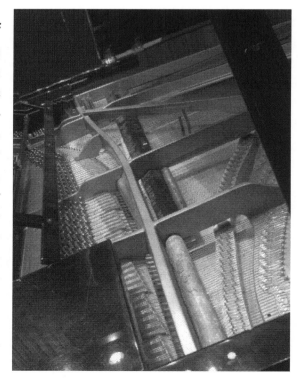

This duet is quite noisy, especially if you use the optional piano preparations.

SIX
"Are you going?" (1997) **triet** 5 minutes

This is somewhat minimalistic, and polyphonic between the three players. It includes a number of sections in which the tempo of one of the pianists gradually speeds up or slows down while the others keep a steady pulse. Like *Raag Gezellig* it is in 7 beats per bar, but unlike *Raag Gezellig* it is fast throughout. The theme is the English folk-melody *Are you going to Scarborough Fair.*

A studio recording (performed by Steven Kings, Daniella Acker and John Pitts) is available from Hyperion/1equalmusic
www.hyperion-records.co.uk/dc.asp?dc=D_1EMIPM08

The first concert performance was at the Kiev "Chamber Music Session" Festival 2010 by the Kiev Piano Duo (Oleksandra Zaytseva & Dmytro Tavanets) with Antoniy Baryshevkiy.

SEVEN
"Experiencing High Volumes" (2014) **triet** 6 minutes

Composed for the Severnside Composers Alliance's second "Three is the Magic Number" concerts of contemporary piano triets at the Lantern, Colston Hall, Bristol in 2014, performed by Milena Zhivotovskaya, Rob Broomfield and John Pitts.

This is pleasant, relaxing armchair music, which doesn't actually get particularly loud. I have Francisco Tárrega (1852-1909) to thank for a motif that recurs through the piece – a short section of his *"Gran Vals"*, which you may recognise. I have omitted the last note of the original melody, which is actually an octave down from a more familiar version you may know. Before this motif made its way into this piece I had considered a title along the lines of *Cycle of Thirds* for harmonic reasons which may be obvious. But I put that idea permanently on hold after trying to get through to a utilities company. In retrospect, I should have ensured that the end looped neatly back to the beginning (which sadly it doesn't quite), so that I could attempt to sell a recording of this piece to businesses for their call waiting music.

Other sheet music available from www.johnpitts.co.uk

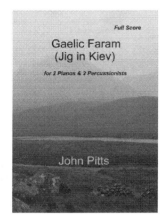

Gaelic Faram (Jig in Kiev) for 2 pianos and 2 percussionists

Designed as a companion piece for Bartok's famous sonata, written for the Kiev Piano Duo for the final concert of the Kiev "Chamber Music Session" Festival 2012. Revised 2016. This is a note-filled, virtuosic piece inspired by British folksong, and includes adaptations of the Dargason jig and the reel Mary Mack, and starts with an attempt to capture some of the ornamented and decorated melody lines typical of Scottish bagpipes.

7 Airs & Fantasias for solo piano (14 pieces)
Toccata "Blue Frenzy" for solo piano
An Autumn Evening for solo piano (3 movements)
A Winter Night for solo piano (3 movements)

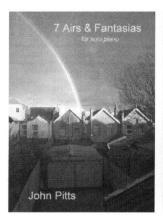
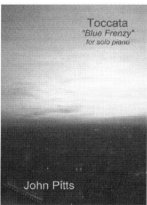

Piano Quartet

Winning piece of the 2003 Philharmonia Orchestra Martin Musical Scholarship Fund Composition Prize at the Royal Festival Hall in London.

Typhoid for piano quartet

Shortlisted piece by the SPNM (Society for the Promotion of New Music) in its original form of Countertenor, Guitar, Violin, Cello, and subsequently performed at an SPNM AGM in its second form for Clarinet, Violin, Cello and Piano. Now in its third instrumentation!

Nuts & Bolts for piano, violin and percussion

Shortlisted piece by the SPNM (Society for the Promotion of New Music)

Cerebrations for string quartet

Reviews of album *Intensely Pleasant Music: 7 Airs & Fantasias and other piano music by John Pitts*

★★★★★
Robert Matthew-Walker, Musical Opinion Magazine

★★★★
Andy Gill, The Independent

"A colossal musical project... stunning and seriously impressive"
John France, MusicWeb International

"Exciting stuff all round - vital, energising, but sensitive when need be. Toes - prepare to tap."
Jonathan Woolf, MusicWeb International

"Realmente un magnífico repertorio desbordante de calidad, belleza y de sumo interés."
★★★★
Alejandro Clavijo, Reviews New Age

"The performances by Steven Kings are excellent ...
All [the pieces] are pleasing to hear and will be satisfying to play"
Patric Standford, Music & Vision Daily

"This is a colorful and interesting set by a talented composer....
The playing by Steven Kings is technically and emotionally perfect."
Oleg Ledeniov, MusicWeb International

★★★★
Stephen Eddins, All Music Guide

"great character and emotional integrity...a thoroughly worthwhile project"
Mark Tanner, Piano Professional Magazine

"recomendable"
Adolfo del Brezo, OpusMusica.com (Spain)

"...surely more than just `intensely pleasant music'."
Michael Darvell, ClassicalSource.com

★★★★
Paul Riley, Venue Magazine

"...highly listenable stuff, very deftly in control of its chosen medium. A number of disparate influences are on display here, but welded into an overall idiom of considerable charm...
`Intensely pleasant music'? Most certainly."
Calum MacDonald, International Record Review Magazine

9/10 *"this album is beautiful, moving and relaxing"*
Andy Whitehead, Cross Rhythms

www.johnpitts.co.uk

Changes

for twenty nifty fingers at a piano

John Pitts
Bristol 1995

12

Passacaglia in C

for piano duet

John Pitts
2000-2012

Keep out of the way!

III

IV

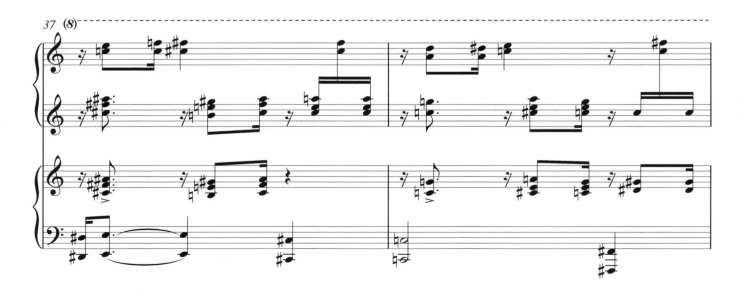

Make space - lean right!

triumphant

triumphant

VI

24

XIII

V.S.

XVIII

40

Raag Gezellig

for 20 jaldi oonglee (20 nifty fingers)

Composed for the Preliminary stage of the
6th International Valberg Competition for Piano Four Hands

John Pitts
2011

(Secondo: independently maintain slightly slower tempo primo, ***ppp*** sempre, completely ignore player Primo)

Primo: ♩. = 54 As if improvised (follow rhythms precisely, but sounding fluid and free)

44

GAT

Very strict time, Tempo Giusto throughout
♩ = 116 **(Never get slower at all, until end)**

Clear and crisp, with mechanical drive, lots of energy and urgency from the start, very dynamic!

(Not too much pedal - half-pedal if needed - but not too little pedal)

(ped. sim. - twice per bar)

Turn page quickly

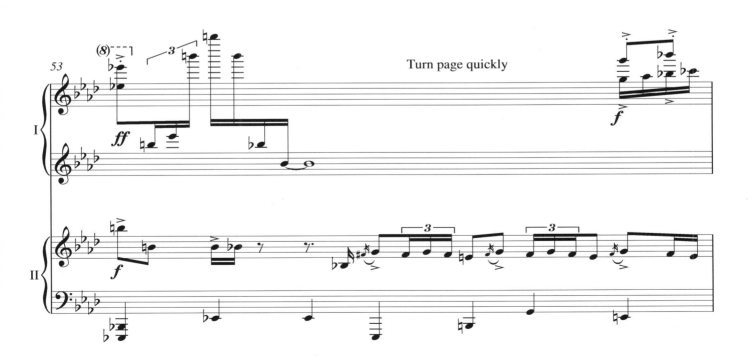

(sempre tempo giusto...............

.............................)

Turn page quickly

56

Turn page quickly

Together

64

(sempre tempo giusto.........)
♩ = 124

JHALA

(still fairly liberal with sustain pedal)

66

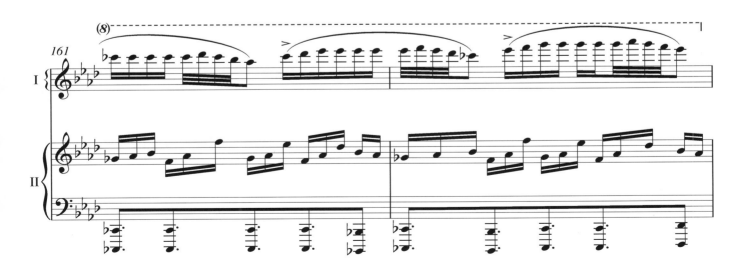

poco a poco accel. _ _ _ _ _ _ _ _ _ _ _ _ _ _ _ _

7 Piano Duets & Triets Copyright © John Pitts 2016

Optional preparations

None of these preparations are even slightly necessary, as "Joyful Balaphony" was written without them. However, they may add some colour and general fun to proceedings.

If you do use them, the aim is to make the piano sound more percussive and give different parts of the piano different timbres. The more you can make the piano sound like a balafon (an African xylophone), and djembe drums, the better.

The following are only suggestions, but every piano and every performing venue is different, so if you do choose to 'prepare' the piano then you'll need to experiment. If there is a rule, which there clearly isn't, it is to try to keep each of the four pitch areas (notated below) sounding a little distinct from each other, and the tone similar across each note of its group. Every pitch needs to be audible, but ideally the timbres of each group should be distinct.

You may need to find ways of keeping things in place. The metal ruler, I find, is extremely effective at altering tone. Get a 12-inch metal ruler, bend it into a curve) - and place it on the relevant strings. If it bounces around or moves too much in performance, you may need to tape paper clips or similar to the ends in order to clip it to particular strings.

On an upright piano things can be slightly trickier, but still do-able. The bent metal ruler will need to be wedged into place, probably using a small cardboard box. As newspaper cannot simply be laid onto the strings, you may need to use a few sheets of normal A4 printer paper which is slightly firmer, roll it up and wedge it into place between the strings and the casing or the frame. If your piano is old and on its way out, and if and only if you are its legal owner, and if you so choose, you could put drawing pins on the hammers of one of the groups. This will of course cause irreparable damage.

Enjoy.

Bright, metallic, bell-like.
On a grand piano, place a bent metal ruler on its thin side over these notes.
All the pitches should be clearly audible.

Snare-drummy / buzzy.
On a grand piano, place a thick folded newspaper over these notes.
All the pitches should be clearly audible.

Percussive / wooden.
On a grand piano, use a wooden clothes peg near the bottom of each string, or wedge small pieces of wood between the strings. All the pitches should be clearly audible.

Metallic, maybe slightly rattley.
On a grand piano, place a bent metal ruler on its thin side over these notes, or wedge thick screws in between the strings. All the pitches should be audible.

Joyful Balaphony

pour Émilie Carcy et Matthieu Millischer
Festival Prospective 22ème siècle, Perpignan, France, 11 Mars 2015

John Pitts
2013

Vibrant, full of energy and attack, exuberant, bright, like an African balafon, every note firm and percussive.
Always smiling.

Free tempo (♩ = c.66), use rhythms as guideline only
Tremelos as fast as possible, with some overlap between hands

Percussive!

Before the start - hold down these notes silently

(Pedal permanently half-down)

(Keep pedal half-down)

Tremelos will subsequently be written with a Z through the stem. Ie: play bar 3 like bar 2.

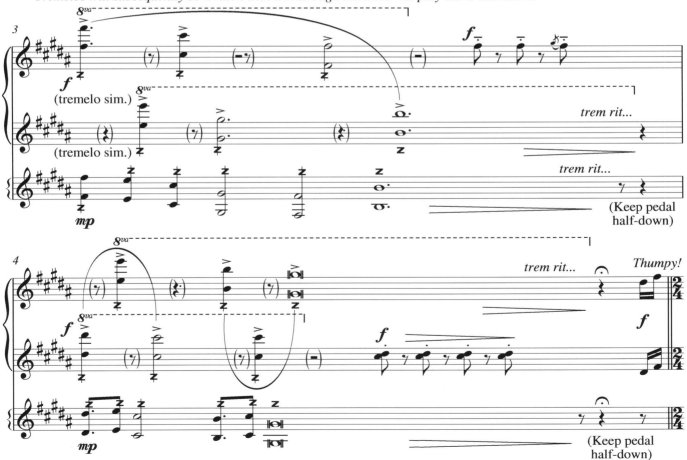

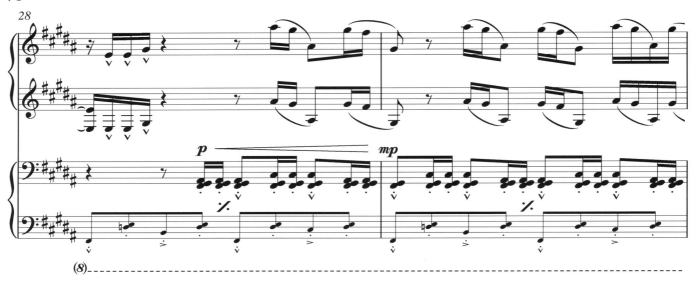

84

Turn quickly!

94

Turn quickly!

98

(♩ = 120)

Glittering Gamelan
for 20 very nifty fingers

Optional piano preparations

None of the following preparations are even slightly necessary, as "Glittering Gamelan" was written without them. However, they may add some colour and general fun to proceedings. If you do use them, the aim is to make the piano sound more percussive and metallic - ie more like a real Gamelan orchestra. The more you can make the piano sound like gongs and metal pots, and the odd drum, the better.

The following are only suggestions, but every piano and every performing venue is different, so if you do choose to 'prepare' the piano then you'll need to experiment. Every pitch should be audible, but ideally the timbres of each group should be distinct.

Bottom A up 9 notes to B - percussive, drummy sound - use a wooden clothes peg near the bottom of each string, or wedge small pieces of wood between the strings. All the pitches should be clearly audible.

Then the C up through the rest of the piano needs to be metallic - bell-like. Metal rulers, I find, are extremely effective at altering tone. Get several 12-inch metal rulers, bend each one into a curve) - and rest them on all these strings. You may need to find ways of keeping things in place. If they bounce around or move too much in performance, you could tape paper clips or similar to the ends in order to clip them to particular strings. Another option is small metal saucepan lids...

Plus, the C above middle C, plus the D and F# above that - these 3 notes can have an additional percussive sound by wedging a piece of wood between 2 of the 3 strings of each note.

On an upright piano things can be slightly trickier, but still do-able. The bent metal rulers will need to be wedged into place, probably using small cardboard boxes. If your piano is old and dying, and if and only if you are its legal owner, and if you so choose, you could put drawing pins on the hammers. This will of course cause <u>irreparable damage</u>.

Glittering Gamelan

for 20 very nifty fingers (on a piano)

an encore for Thorson and Thurber, Samsø Piano Festival 2014

Inspired by "Gamelan Balaganjur" - literally *"Gamelan of Walking Warriors"* - a type
of Indonesian band of dancers and musicians originally existing as a military band, but now
known for competition performances which display incredibly elaborate, through-composed
pieces that require enormous ensemble skill to cope with the complex rhythmic gestures
and ever changing speeds.

John Pitts
2014

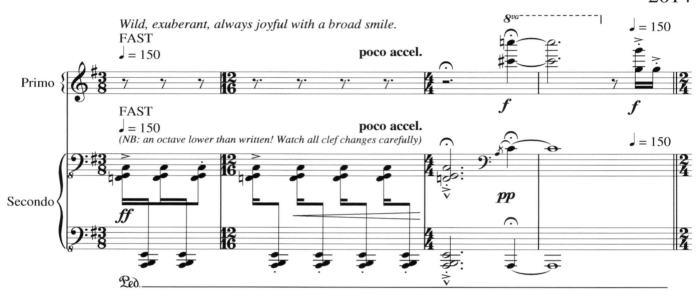

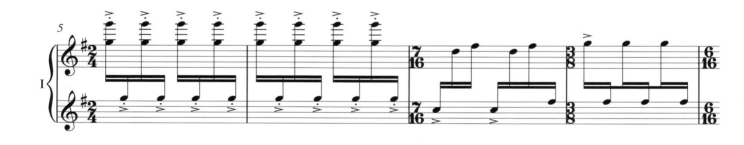

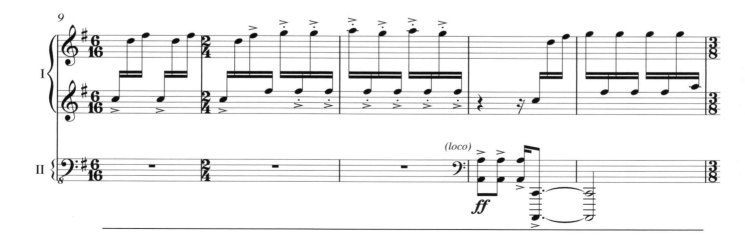

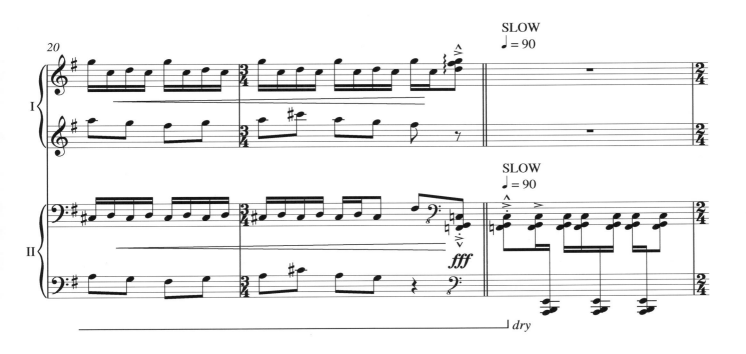

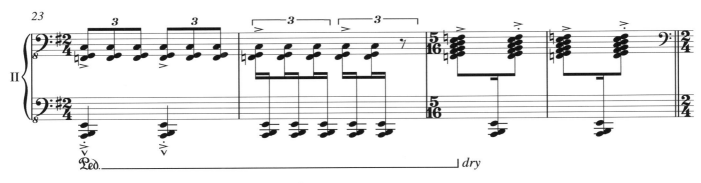

108

(sounding rhythmically free)

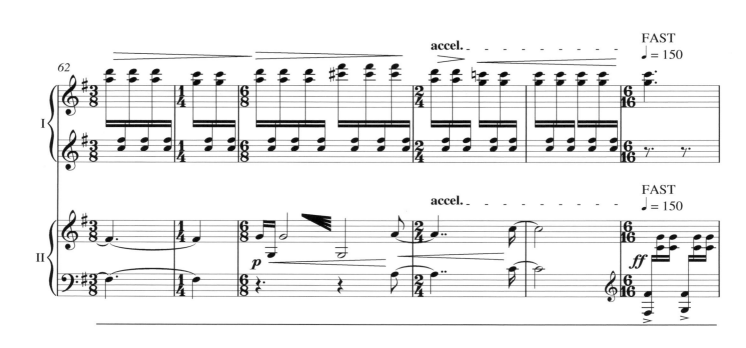

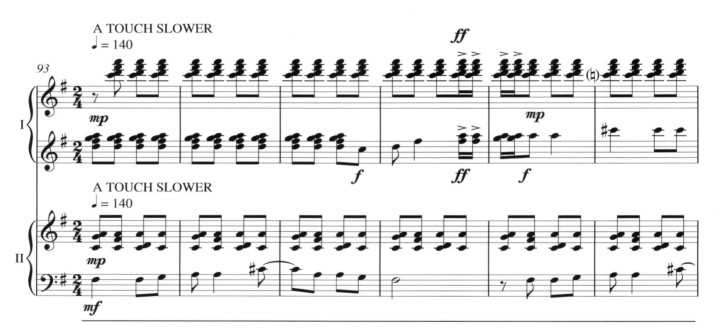

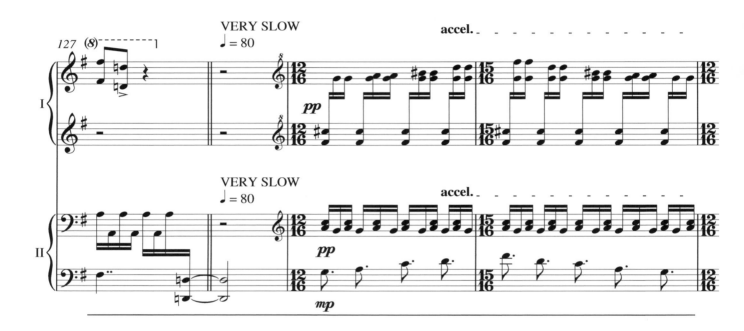

Are you going?

for thirty nifty fingers at a piano

John Pitts
Bristol 1997

122

128

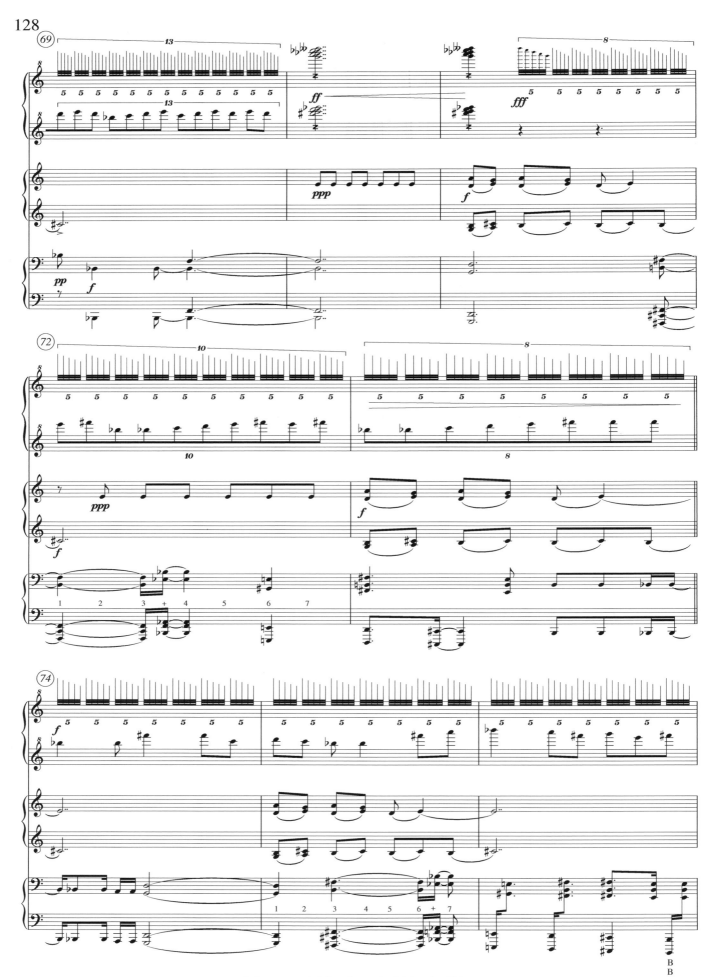

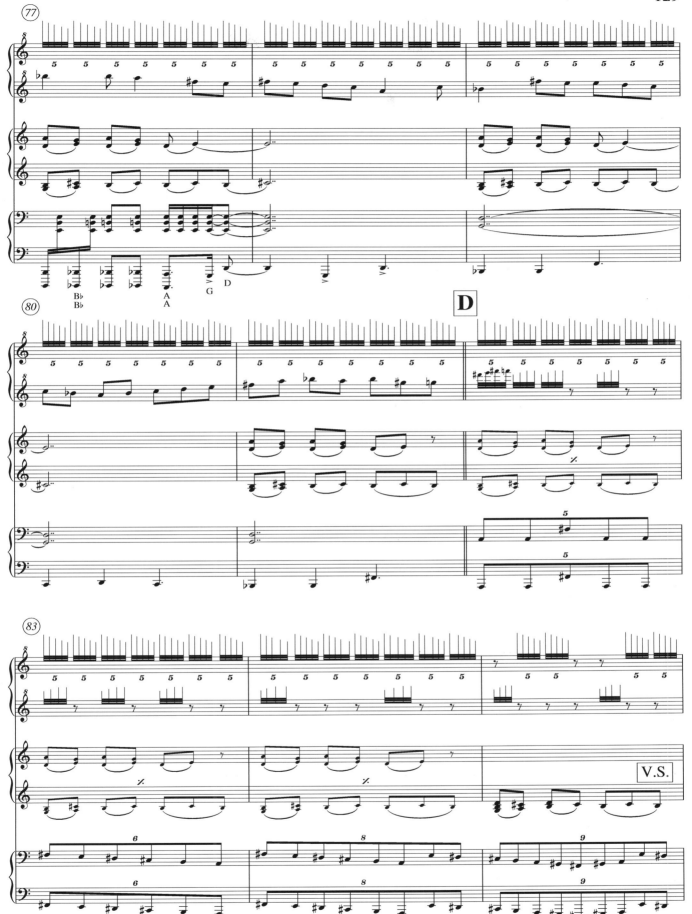

Experiencing High Volumes

for Piano Triet

John Pitts
2014
(Revised 2016)

Francisco Tárrega (1852-1909) "Gran Vals"

136

1

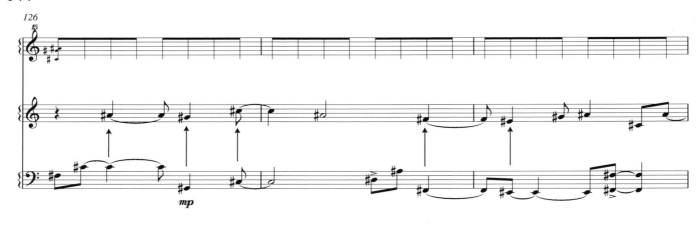

Printed in Great Britain
by Amazon